CALM DOWN AND RELAX
COLOR THE CLASSICS
FAMILY FOCUS DOUBLE PAGE EDITION
AUTHOR L.I. OLSON
VOLUME TWO EDITION ONE

A special Thanks to the wonderful illustrators of the 19th and 20th centuries such as
L. Leslie Brook, Randolph Caldecott, and Norman Rockwell among others whose beautiful
works inspired me to do these coloring pages. I sincerely hope that coloring together becomes
a tool for better relationships between family members and friends.
Addional books may be purchased or individual pages downloaded by going to our website:
premiumcoloringbooks.com
Thank you for purchasing our book.
L.I. Olson,
Coloring Book Illustrator

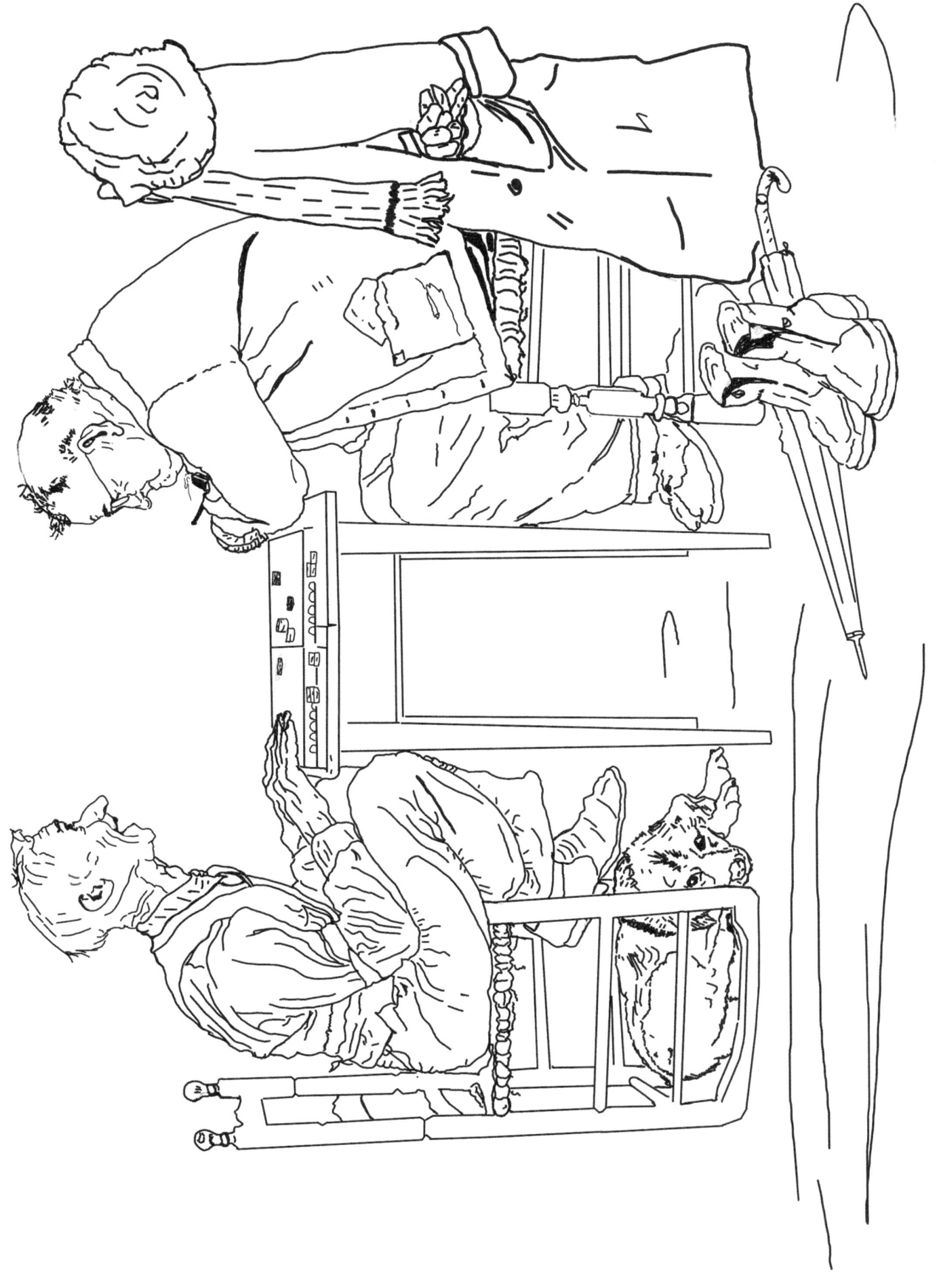

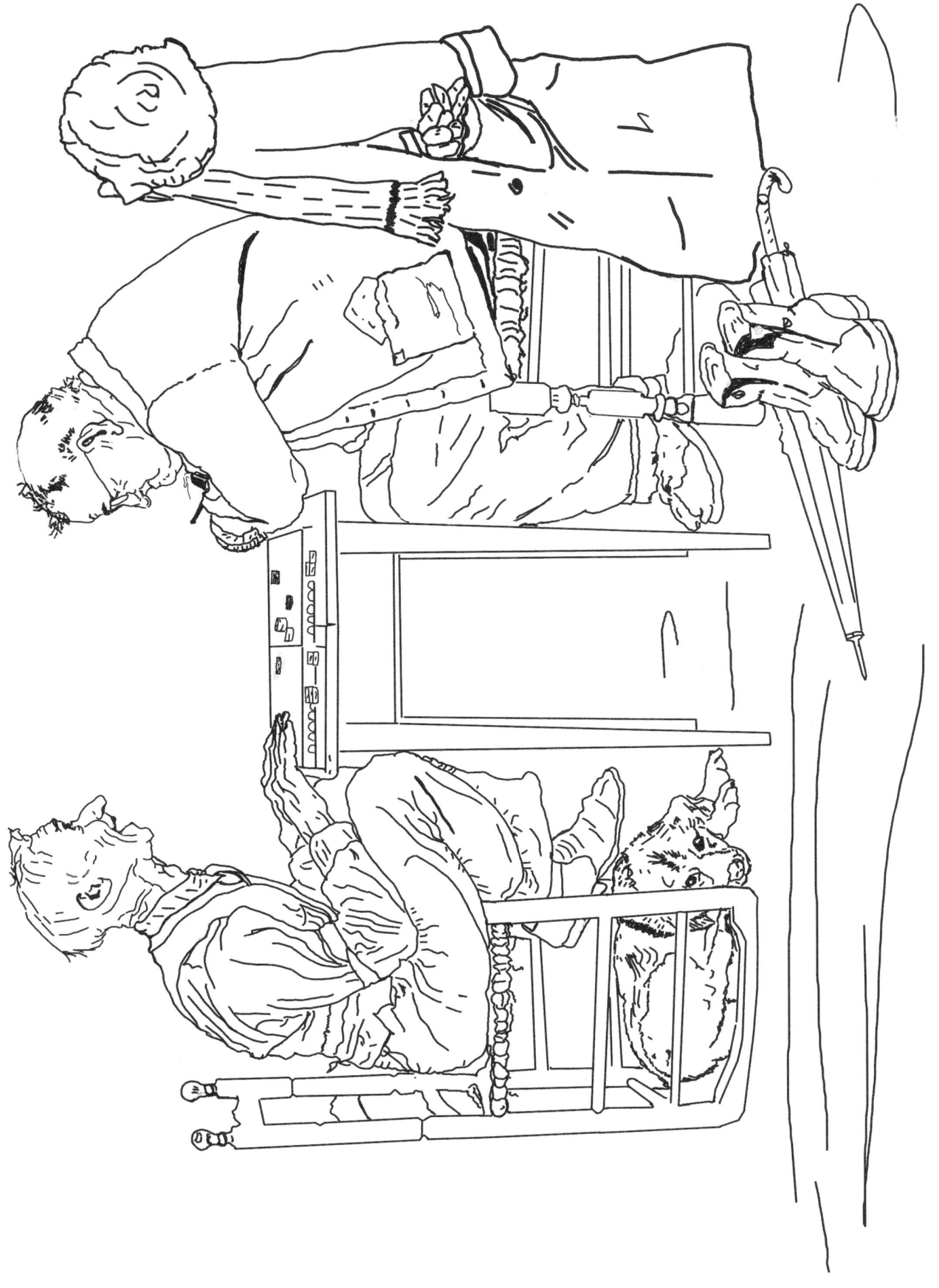

May 12

Jan. 3

October 26

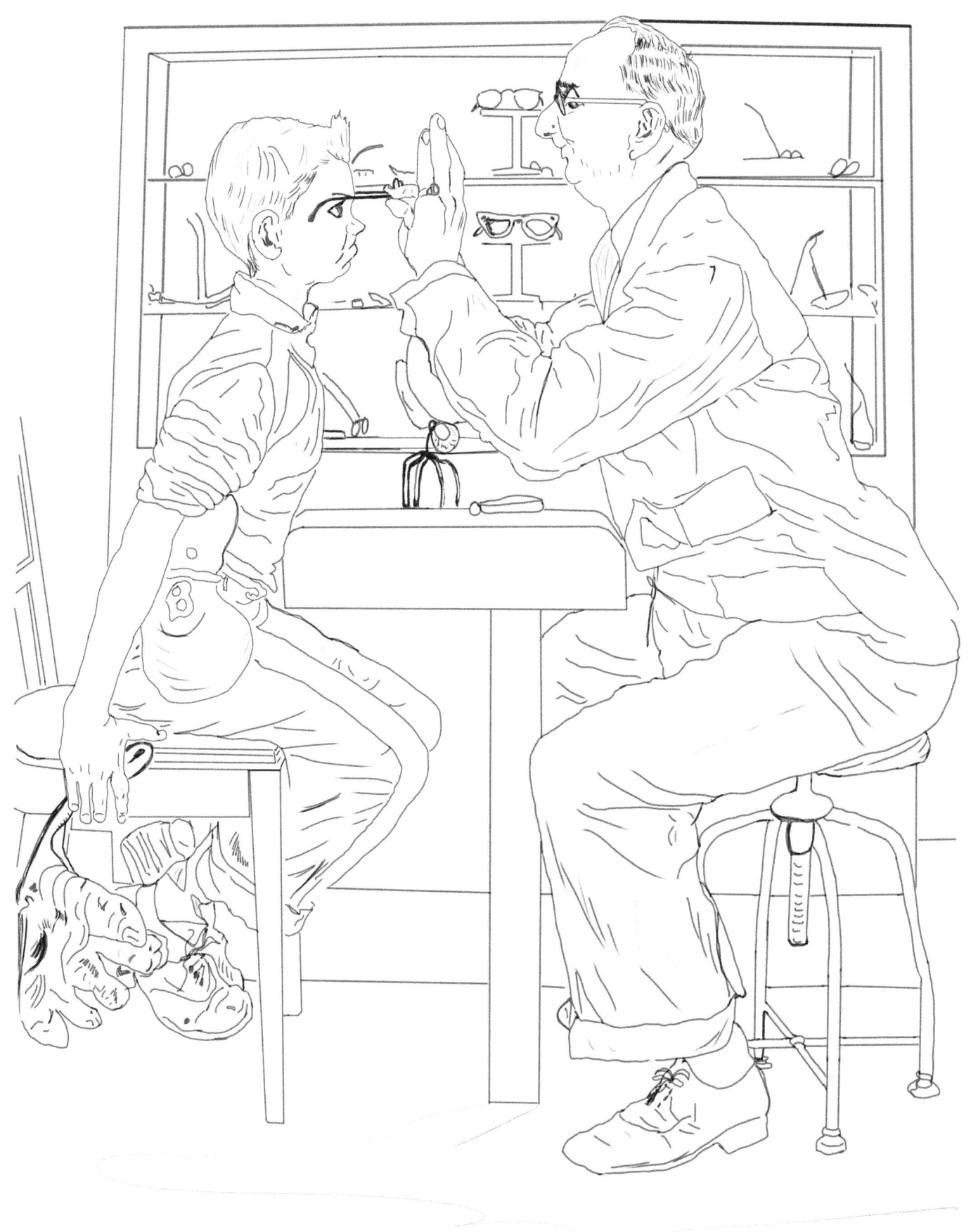